Coping with

CEREBRAL PALSY

Laura Anne Gilman

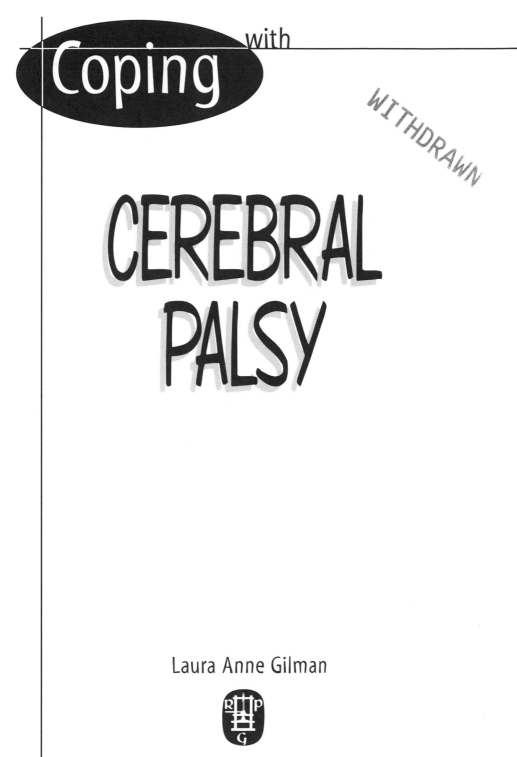

The Rosen Publishing Group, Inc.
New York

Published in 2001 by The Rosen Publishing Group
29 East 21st Street, New York, NY 10010

Copyright © 2001 by The Rosen Publishing Group, Inc.

First Edition

Cover © Tom Nebbia/Corbis

Library of Congress Cataloging-in-Publication Data

Gilman, Laura Anne.
Coping with cerebral palsy / by Laura Anne Gilman.—1st ed.
p. cm. — (Coping)
Includes bibliographical references and index.
ISBN 0-8239-3150-1
1. Cerebral palsy—Juvenile literature. 2. Cerebral palsied
children—Juvenile literature. [1. Cerebral palsy.] I. Title.
II. Series.
RJ496.C4 G53 2001
362.1'9892836—dc21

2001001390

Manufactured in the United States of America

Contents

Introduction

Cerebral palsy. You've dealt with it for your entire life, from the moment you first became aware you were different from other kids—and yet, somehow, now that you're a teenager, it's worse. All you want to do right now is fit in, be part of the group. And you can't. No matter what you do, they know. You're different. Your body doesn't move right, and you're never sure if it will obey your commands.

And now, more than ever before, it matters. Your life is changing, your body is changing, and everything's confused. At times, you may want to give up, give in, and make it all go away. But there are also going to be some wonderful years ahead of you. Exciting experiences. Fascinating discoveries. And having cerebral palsy shouldn't stop you from having any of them.

"Yeah, yeah," you're saying. "I've heard that before." Parents, teachers, doctors, therapists, overly inquisitive relatives—they've all been in your face. They might have been sympathetic or bracing, compassionate or just annoying, or all of the above, at one time or another. And there are probably days when you would like nothing better than to banish them—and their well-meaning advice—out the door.

It's okay to be angry, or depressed, or wonder why this had to happen to you. In fact, probably the most commonly spoken phrase in the history of the human race has been "Why me?" And since the damage that causes cerebral palsy typically occurs before you have any control whatsoever over your life, this question can have an extra weight for you. "What did I do to deserve this?" can't be answered when you didn't do anything. In almost every case, there's no finger to point and no one to say, "This is all your fault." And if there were—what good would it do? Blame doesn't change anything.

So, yes, "Why me?" is a fair question. And yes, you have the right to be angry about it, to feel like you got a raw deal. But don't let yourself get too tied up in it. Just as blame doesn't change anything, neither does regret or bitterness. It's far better to look forward, not back. To quote a very wise woman named Carla whom I know only from the Internet, "I may have cerebral palsy, but it doesn't have me."

Remember, you're not alone. According to United Cerebral Palsy, a nationwide network founded in 1949, more than 500,000 children and adults in the United States have one or more symptoms of cerebral palsy. Almost 5,000 babies and infants are diagnosed each year despite increased medical vigilance during pregnancy. And because of that, there's also a widespread support network for people with cerebral palsy. If you want a formal organization, it exists. If you're looking for something a little more casual, it's only as far away as a phone call or an Internet connection.

No, this book isn't going to tell you that you're just like everyone else. You're not. You have cerebral palsy, and that fact alone will color almost every aspect of your life. But that doesn't mean that it has to define you.

Yes, you're going to have to deal with hurdles that other kids won't face. And you may have to work a little harder, reach a little farther, to participate in everyday life. You'll also have questions that other kids don't need to ask, and you'll probably have a lot of anger and resentment as well. It's okay. Don't deny those feelings—but don't let them rule you, either. Again, you're not alone. Not only are there other people out there who understand what you're going through, but there's a lot of help—from people like you, who've grown up with cerebral palsy, as well as from medical professionals—out there as well. All you have to do is look for it.

This book is here to help you. Think of it as a practical guide to living, as opposed to just getting by. It's for you to read on your own, and for you to share with your friends, your siblings, your boyfriend or girlfriend, your bunk mate at camp, or your roomie in college. We're going to cover the basics, dispel a few myths, clarify a couple of misconceptions. And we'll get into the gritty details, including medical facts, social nuances, legal aids, and practical advice on school, work, dating—yes, even sex.

You can read this book straight through. Or you can flip around from chapter to chapter, finding the stuff that's important to you. There are no rules here. This is your book. Use what you need. Talk about what you read. And don't ever forget that this is just a starting point.

Famous People with Physical or Speech Difficulties

Ludwig van Beethoven, Composer
Joseph Biden, U.S. Congressman
John Callahan, Cartoonist
Lewis Carroll, Author
Winston Churchill, Former Prime Minister of Britain
Chuck Close, Artist
Walter Cronkite, Journalist
Chris Fonseca, Comedian
Stephen Hawking, Astrophysicist
Joseph Heller, Author
John Hockenberry, Journalist
James Earl Jones, Actor
Helen Keller, Author
Ron Kovic, Disability Advocate
Marlee Matlin, Actress
Itzhak Perlman, Violinist
Christopher Reeve, Actor
Janet Reno, Former U.S. Attorney General
Franklin Delano Roosevelt, Former President of the United States
Carly Simon, Singer
Richard Thomas, Actor
John Updike, Author
Heather Whitestone, Former Miss America
Frank Wolf, U.S. Congressman
Adapted from a chart from the Council on Exceptional Children

Cerebral Palsy:
The Basics

Who You Are

Cerebral: an adjective, meaning "of the brain." Palsy: a noun, meaning paralysis, especially with involuntary tremors.

"Sure," you're thinking. "Tell me something I don't know." It's true, you've heard the words for your entire life. You may have done research on it, determined to know everything there is to know, or you may have simply absorbed the basic details from your parents or your doctor. If your symptoms are mild enough, you may even have tried to ignore it and pretend it didn't affect you, probably with less than wonderful results. Cerebral palsy, CP, doesn't go away, and it can't be cured—yet. With recent advances in genome typing, our understanding of the human body is expanding rapidly, and almost anything is possible in the near future.

It's important to remember that cerebral palsy isn't one specific problem, but rather a wide range of physical difficulties caused by damage to the portions of the brain that control motor function, placed under one all-encompassing label. There is no easy generalization to make on the subject.

Cerebral palsy is a disorder you have; it isn't you. There's nothing more important you can take away from this book than that deceptively simple fact. You are more than legs that don't work right, a tongue and jaw that have trouble forming words properly, or any other specific attribute or symptom. You're a person, with wants and needs and dreams. And you have every right to express them, and follow up on them, and—in short—live.

Sarah is twenty. She has been in a wheelchair for her entire life. Her legs are effectively useless—she calls them "shoe holders"—and she has epilepsy in addition to cerebral palsy. Despite all of this, she will graduate from college next year with a degree in art history. Sarah plans to open an interior-decorating service with her cousin, who has been her strongest supporter from day one. "We understand each other; encourage each other; abuse each other, too—I take my share of abuse. But when I wanted to give up, because it was just too much to keep going day after day, he was my best cheerleader. He knew I could do it. And he never let me give up."

FACT: Cerebral palsy isn't a disease. It's not contagious, and it's not hereditary.

FACT: Cerebral palsy isn't progressive; the damage done to your brain is not going to get worse as you get older.

FACT: Cerebral palsy doesn't always involve learning disabilities, much less severe retardation.

FACT: Nobody has ever died of cerebral palsy.

FACT: Cerebral palsy is nothing to be ashamed of.

The rest of this chapter is going to be a refresher course on the basics of cerebral palsy: what it is, related conditions, how it can be treated, and what you can continue to do to improve your quality of life on both a short-term and long-term basis. You can, of course, skip this section—but it won't take long, and you may pick up some information that comes in handy down the road, either for yourself or for use in explaining cerebral palsy to someone else. In fact, you might want to leave this book lying around where your friends might pick it up. A little education goes a long way toward breaking down barriers, be they physical, mental, or emotional.

Causes and Symptoms

Every baby who comes into the world faces a gamut of tests to determine its health, especially if there were complications during the birth or during the pregnancy itself. So when you were born, the doctors may have known there was damage from the first moment, based on visual examination and your Apgar score. Or it may not have become apparent until your first birthday or even a little later, depending on how your particular symptoms manifested.

But unlike the more obvious birth defects, such as blindness or a deformed hand or foot, cerebral palsy isn't easily diagnosed. Remember, it's not a single

7

symptom, but a grouping of difficulties caused by pre- or postnatal damage to the portions of the brain that affect and control physical movement. It's a little like giving an order to a waiter who doesn't know how to get to the kitchen. There's a talented chef waiting—but the food never gets made.

And because the brain is such a delicately tuned machine, when one thing is affected, so too are others. Related problems seen in people with cerebral palsy include epilepsy, vision and hearing difficulties, and varying degrees of learning disabilities. All of these, of course, also occur in people without cerebral palsy. In fact, learning disabilities affect a large portion of the population without any physical difficulties at all, and are in many ways the most difficult—and most frustrating— hurdle you may face. These are discussed in further detail later in this chapter.

"But why," you may wonder. "Why me?"

The truth is, there are many different causes of cerebral palsy. If a woman is exposed to an infectious disease like rubella (German measles) early in her pregnancy; if an infant doesn't get enough oxygen during labor; if Rh incompatibility occurs; if an infection sets in during the first few days of a newborn's life; if there is damage done to the child in the first few months of life—the list goes on and on. Despite all the advances modern medicine has made recently, the brain is still quite mysterious, and the brain of a developing infant is the most mysterious thing of all. Despite the best care and the most stringent precautions, CP still does happen, and the precise cause often remains unknown.

Doctors split the 'types' of cerebral palsy into four different categories:

Spastic

Spasticity means stiffness or tightness of muscles. The muscles are stiff because the message to them is relayed incorrectly through the damaged part of the brain. When people without cerebral palsy perform a voluntary movement, some groups of muscles become tighter and some groups of muscles relax, according to a series of directives from the brain. With spastic cerebral palsy, the directives are scrambled, and both groups of muscles may become tighter, which makes the movement difficult, or impossible. This is the most common type of cerebral palsy.

Athetoid

A lack of coordination and uncontrolled involuntary movements are the main symptoms here. Generally, they're most notable when you initiate a movement—as though the order to move was received, but the muscle somehow "forgot" how to do it. Your muscles may be very weak, or feel "floppy" no matter how hard you try to control them.

Ataxic

This is the least common type of cerebral palsy. Ataxia is the word used for unsteady, shaky movements or tremors. It can also mess with your balance and depth perception.

Mixed

Often, several different types may be diagnosed. The term for this, simply enough, is "mixed."

In some more severe cases, the damage that causes cerebral palsy may also cause related difficulties with bladder and bowel control, breathing problems, skin disorders, and learning disabilities. You may also suffer from seizures, hearing or visual impairment, and learning disorders, which are discussed below. While one or more of these may affect a person with cerebral palsy, they occur in people without cerebral palsy as well. If you have one of these additional symptoms, there are treatments and support groups specifically for them.

Cerebral palsy is also often classified by the portions of the body affected.

Diplegia refers to both arms and legs being affected.

Monoplegia refers to only one limb (a leg or an arm) being affected. This is the rarest of the five categories.

Quadriplegia refers to the entire body being affected, including the face and trunk.

Hemiplegia refers to only one side of the body being affected, much like a stroke victim might lose control over half of his or her body.

Triplegia refers to three limbs being affected. This is almost as rare as monoplegia.

In all likelihood, you won't have any need to know these terms in your daily life. But knowing them and knowing your own particular specifics will make it easier for you to take your condition in hand. You're not a kid anymore and you need to know and understand your treatment so that you can make informed decisions for yourself.

Yes, you're still a minor, and your parents still have the power to make decisions for you—but they won't always.

And even before the law says you have final say, you should be discussing these options with your parents or guardians. A major part of taking control of your own life involves making decisions about medicines and treatments, and you don't want to be caught by surprise once the time comes for you to have the final say.

Learning Disabilities

As mentioned earlier, this discussion is important enough to merit its own section. If cerebral palsy is caused by damage to the brain, does that mean people with cerebral palsy are mentally impaired?

Yes, some people with cerebral palsy are mentally impaired. But it's not an A=B equation. Statistics say that perhaps 35 to 40 percent of those with CP can be classified as mentally impaired. However, it is more common for someone with cerebral palsy to have a learning disorder, which is not the same thing as being mentally impaired. If you have a learning disability, it doesn't mean you're stupid. In fact, many people with learning disabilities are actually of above-average intelligence. However, your brain may process information differently, making it hard for you to learn by traditional methods.

According to the U.S. Department of Education, about 17.5 percent of children in the United States will encounter a problem learning to read during the first three years in school.

According to the *Journal of Pediatrics*, about 2 to 6.5 percent of children in the United States will encounter a serious problem with their math skills during elementary school.

Those figures are for the entire population, not just people with cerebral palsy! Every year, 120,000 additional students are found to have learning disabilities, a diagnosis now shared by 2.4 million schoolchildren in the United States.

There are several recognized forms of learning disabilities, among them dyslexia, processing deficits, developmental aphasia, and dyscalculia. You may also encounter the following terms: attention deficit disorder (ADD), attention deficit hyperactivity disorder (ADHD), dyslexia visual processing disorders, audio processing disorders, and communication disorders. While not technically learning disabilities, they do often appear in tandem with them and are commonly referred to as such.

Symptoms of these conditions include:

⮑ Difficulty completing tasks; giving up easily because of frustration

⮑ Difficulty remembering facts or a list of items

⮑ Difficulty following oral and/or written directions

⮑ Confusion trying to follow more than one direction at a time

⮑ Difficulty staying on task; being easily distracted

⮑ Difficulty making decisions

⮑ Overimpulsiveness

⮑ Poor sense of time

⮑ Difficulty recalling information from memory

If you do have a learning disability, you may spend a great deal of time berating yourself for being stupid, for not "getting" something that's obviously so easy. You may contemplate giving up on whatever is causing you difficulty. I know because I have a learning disability, too: dyscalculia, which means I have difficulty processing numbers and numerical concepts. But that hasn't stopped me, mainly because I'm too stubborn to give up. And, often, that's all it takes to break through the wall of a learning disability—a determined refusal to stop trying.

The important thing to remember is that while having a learning disability will create long-term problems for you, it's something that you can learn to work around. Therapy, training, patience, and most of all an understanding of what's wrong are powerful tools. Don't ever discount them.

Being Positive and Proactive

Diagnosing cerebral palsy in infants is difficult, even with today's hypersensitive medical technology, and we still have no cure. Fortunately for you, the methods of managing it are more advanced, and new ones are being developed every year. Some of them, admittedly, are more effective than others, and some may be the modern equivalent of snake oil and "quack" tonics. Before you try any new "guaranteed cure," be sure that you discuss it with your doctor and parents. And if you have Internet access, check out http://www.quackwatch.com before doing anything else! They're constantly on the lookout for treatments that sound too good to be true.

Even if it has a proven record of success, not every program is for everyone, and some may not be practical for you. But here is a listing of some of the more widely used techniques for controlling and reducing the effects of cerebral palsy. Just remember, if you don't feel good about a treatment, odds are it won't be effective for you. Mental attitude is more than half the battle.

Physical Therapy

This is one of the classic treatments for cerebral palsy, and as such you're probably already familiar with it. Physical therapy (also called neuro-developmental treatment) is used to decrease spasticity, strengthen the underlying muscles, and train the body into proper motor patterns. A good physical therapist will also teach you how to continue the exercises on your own, if possible. The Neuro-Developmental Treatment Association Web site (http://www.ndta.org) has more detailed information on the practices.

Speech and Language Therapy

Communication is the key to connecting with the rest of the world. It can be horribly frustrating if you're unable to explain to someone what's going on with your body, or in your head. Some speech therapists have additional training as oral motor specialists and can help with more immediately serious issues with eating, breathing, swallowing, and oral sensitivity. Improving your control over facial and vocal expressions is also a huge step toward better self-esteem.

Drug Therapy

Your doctor may have prescribed drugs if you suffer from seizures. Any medication will be tailored to your specific needs, but often it takes a series of trials before you discover what works best for you, if at all. Drugs are not a quick fix, but used in conjunction with other treatments, they can take you a long way toward controlling your body.

Regular Vision and Hearing Examinations

Sounds simple, doesn't it? You spend so much time in your doctor's office, there's no way that you could have missed those. But it can't be stressed enough how important it is to have your eyes and ears checked on a regular basis by certified professionals. There are many visual problems, like steregnosia and strabismus, which are associated with cerebral palsy. Even if your eyes are otherwise fine, something as simple—and as common—as trouble with your ability to gauge depth perception could be a problem: Missing a step might have more serious consequences than expected if your reflexes don't compensate in time.

Hearing is another thing we take for granted. But it's a major part of how we deal with and interact in the world every day. Think about it: If you have trouble hearing a particular sound, your understanding of those around you may be hampered. And without a hearing test, you would never even know that there was a problem.

And don't think, just because you were fitted with a hearing aid or were told you didn't need glasses, that's all it takes. A person with visual difficulty, even something as commonplace as nearsightedness, might go through five or six prescriptions in a lifetime—or her prescription might change every year. And hearing loss is sometimes so subtle that it goes unrecognized, unless specifically tested.

Feldenkrais
This is a body awareness methodology that can help you master control of your body. Talk to your doctor about this, or log onto the Web site of The Feldenkrais Guild at http://www.healthy.net/feldenkrais for more information.

Hippotherapy
Otherwise known as horseback riding, this is typically done at an accredited facility with animals that have been specifically trained for this. The physical benefits of horseback riding are numerous: The horse's movement

increases your sense of balance, and sitting properly in a saddle stretches your legs and aids your posture. Plus, it's just fun. Never underestimate the power of having a good time.

If this isn't an option for you, because of costs or availability or allergies, you might want to try bicycling. There are specially adapted bicycles and adult tricycles that can be adjusted to your requirements. You can read more about this in chapter two.

Swimming

Odds are, you've spent a great deal of time in a pool already, especially if your mobility is strictly limited on land. Exercises are easier and often are more effective when your weight is supported by water, and a slightly higher-than-usual temperature can also help your muscles to relax rather than freeze up. Swimming also strengthens the parts of your body that aren't affected by cerebral palsy, making sure that you keep an overall tone to your muscles.

Botox

The treatment involves receiving injections of botulism toxin in minute amounts, effectively "paralyzing" the spastic muscle, giving the nonspastic muscles a chance to strengthen. Your doctor will typically use botox on one muscle group in order to affect a specific action such as independent walking.

Since the effects wear off after a few months, botox injections are not considered a long-term fix for orthopedic problems but may be used as a reliable way to delay or minimize the need for surgery.

Electrical Stimulation

Electrodes are placed on the skin over the muscle group or groups that need treatment, and very low levels of electrical current are used to stimulate the muscles to contract. Therapeutic electrical stimulation (TES) is administered at night while you sleep. It has been proven to add more muscle fiber, but exercise and/or physical therapy is a must, in order to make the most of that growth.

Hyberbaric Oxygen Therapy

It is also called HBO or HBOT. In this treatment, you receive pure oxygen through repeated sessions in a pressurized tank. The theory is that it stimulates or restores function to nerve cells that border the area of the brain that has been damaged.

Of course, this is only a brief listing of all the choices that are out there, and even more will no doubt be in testing phases or will be approved for your use by the time this book is in print. Managing cerebral palsy, like any other lifelong condition, isn't a matter of quick fixes or miracle cures. There is no cure for cerebral palsy—yet. But the human body is a work in progress, and the more you do, the more you'll discover you can do.

Remember, your teens are a time for testing your boundaries and stretching your reach as far as it can go. It's only normal to fall short or fail to reach your goals occasionally. But if you don't try, you'll never know if that goal was within reach. The words "You can't because you have cerebral palsy" should never be accepted as fact if there's any reasonable chance that you can.

And don't let your parents hold you back, either. If they protest, or you think that they're being too protective, ask your doctor to speak with them about what you want to do, and get his or her assistance in teaching them how to let go, just a little. It won't be easy—they've been protecting you too long to stop just because you tell them to do so. And nothing is going to stop them from worrying. But maybe you can talk them into stepping away, just the same way they had to when you first started school.

And if all else fails, remind them that you are a teenager, after all. You're supposed to drive them crazy!

I Want a
Normal Life!

All of your life you've been different: different body, different classes, different responsibilities. If you were given one wish, out of the blue, no strings attached, odds are pretty good that it would be a simple one—to be normal.

The hard truth is, there is no such thing as a "normal" life—or rather, there are so many definitions of normal that it's almost impossible to be abnormal. But it is possible for you to live within the mainstream: to be a contributing, participating member of society, rather than feeling like an outsider, or, worse, some kind of burden or responsibility on others.

And it's not "someday in the future" that this can happen. It's right now, beginning today.

What Do You Mean, "These Are the Best Years of Your Life"?

Are there days that you're convinced that there's no way you could ever fit in with the rest of your high school, that nobody would ever want you around?

Guess what? Even kids who don't have cerebral palsy are thinking that. The very word "adolescence" conjures up images of troubled teens and maladjusted loners, and not without reason. There are psychiatrists who specialize in the teenage years and make a great deal of money convincing their patients that it is possible to survive junior high and high school.

The years between twelve and twenty are a difficult time. In fact, "horrible" probably covers a lot of it. Your body is going through major hormonal changes, the social structure of your peer group is changing, you can't stand some kids you grew up with anymore, and the kids you once couldn't stand suddenly don't seem so bad. Or maybe you hate everyone and everything.

That's okay. Really. As your parents are often heard to say, it's a phase. It will pass. It's normal for a teenager to feel that way. And there are ways to make the everyday routine easier for yourself.

Independence

Mark claims his mother can't let go. At fourteen, he wants to go out with his friends, hang out after school, watch television, or go to the movies without having to check in every ten minutes. His friends are people he's grown up with, they know what physical assistance he needs, and their parents all know him. It's not as though he's going to get into any trouble. But his mother still has trouble letting go of the child he once was.

"It's like she's still afraid something terrible is going to happen. She's still feeling guilty for doing something

21

'wrong' when I was a baby, I guess. But I'm not a baby. I need her to step away and let me do my thing."

That's what it's all about. Check in any psychology textbook and it will confirm that the early teen years—twelve, thirteen, often even earlier—are when children start to push away from their parents, establish their own independence, and find their own boundaries. Cerebral palsy makes that push for independence more difficult: How can you stand on your own when you may not be able to stand on your own?

The first step, as always, is the most difficult. You have to tell people what you want. That includes your mom and dad. Don't be afraid of hurting their feelings—stifling what you're feeling is worse, in the long run. It may lead to arguments, maybe even out-and-out fights. Don't let that stop you. This isn't a temper tantrum, or an unreasonable demand on your part.

If you think you can't do it, or you suspect it might turn ugly, ask a family friend to step in as a mediator, to keep anyone from saying things he or she would regret. If you know other parents who have gone through this already with their kids, ask them—your parents may listen a little easier to people who have been there before. And you can learn something from how they managed it.

If your cerebral palsy is severe, you may never be able to achieve the "holy grail" of total independence, physically. Don't let that stop you. Independence is less about doing everything for yourself, and more about thinking for yourself. It's making decisions for yourself.

One of the most important things you can do is determine what your problem areas are. Be honest with yourself—but don't be too hard on yourself, either. Is it a physical problem that's creating a barrier between you and independence? If so, what can you do to lessen its restrictions?

One of the worst limitations imposed on teenagers with cerebral palsy used to be transportation. At a time when mobility is so important, the thought of being dependent on someone else to take you anywhere is devastating. But you've got options. Public transport is slowly getting on track with handicapped access, and if your local bus system is not equipped, one large complaint in a public forum—a newspaper, a town council meeting—should be enough to get things jumpstarted. Raise your voice and demand your rights.

If the lure of a driver's license was once just a cruel joke, take another look. It may be that there are adaptations available now that will allow you to drive. They're not cheap, but financial aid may be available. See the Where to Go for Help section at the end of this book.

Also, don't dismiss out of hand the idea of mom, dad, or a sibling driving you around. Yes, it can be embarrassing. But only if you let it. Try working out a bill of transportation rights, specifying the places you need to get to and how often (the mall, the movie theater, the library, etc). Once it's agreed upon, the drivers in your household can work out a schedule that will get you there with a minimum of stress on everyone's part. And, if all else fails, see if the local taxi service in your town would be willing to run a tab for you in case of emergencies.

But for some of you, the feeling of dependence is much more immediate than that. It's about the simple ability to do things for yourself, whether it's getting a snack to eat or something as complicated as working machinery that's not adapted for you. Although you want to be able to do everything on your own, sometimes your body simply won't cooperate.

When you were a kid, your parents did a lot for you. That won't work anymore; you've got your own life to lead. In many cases, an aide can be an invaluable help. But if you're looking for a way to develop more independence, and you fit the guidelines, a service animal might be just the thing. Although the majority of service animals are dogs, other animals and some types of birds have been used successfully.

A service animal may provide some or all of the following assistance: guiding a visually impaired person around obstacles as he travels; alerting a person with a hearing impairment to the presence of specific sounds, both familiar (doorbell, phone, baby crying) and unfamiliar (burglar, emergency sirens); and general assistance.

"General assistance" covers a wide range of help, including mobility (helping you balance, pulling your wheelchair, and helping you get up from a sitting or fallen position), retrieval (getting items that you dropped or that are otherwise out of reach, and carrying items by mouth on command), scent discrimination (locating items, people, places such as bathrooms, elevators, escalators, and a return path), and general aid.

Sounds fantastic? There's more. Trained dogs can open and close doors and drawers, help you dress or undress, carry items in a backpack, act as a physical buffer to jostling by others, put clothes in the washer or dryer and remove them, and bark for help. In addition, a number of dogs have demonstrated the ability to warn their owners of oncoming seizures, enabling the owners to position themselves safely.

And, overall, service animals provide a familiar, loving presence during times of stress, allowing their owners to remain calm and healthy. After all, how could life not be all right if there's an animal waiting to tell you how much he loves you via application of tongue to face, or a muzzle thrust into your hand? Animals have perfected the art of unconditional love.

But before you decide that a service animal is the right choice for you, ask yourself the following questions:

- ↩ Do you have the ability to care for a service animal's basic needs, like grooming, petting, and feeding?

- ↩ Will your physical condition improve if a service animal performs basic tasks for you?

- ↩ Would having a service animal help you be more active physically?

- ↩ Would an animal help you socially by creating a means of interaction with others?

- ↩ Would the animal's presence reassure your parents that you're not alone or helpless, thereby reducing some of the stress in your family life?

If you think the answer to most or all of the above questions is yes, then maybe a service animal is the right choice for you. But remember, you would be taking on the responsibility for another creature's life, and that's not a decision to be made lightly.

If you still want to go ahead with this, trained service animals can be obtained through special programs, or you and a trainer can choose and train an animal. Programs may require a person to meet specific disability requirements, and there might be a waiting period before an animal is available.

And yes, you can take your service animal with you everywhere, even into a restaurant. Asking for a chair for the animal may be pushing it, however!

But not all barriers are physical ones. There may be other things that are making your parents uncomfortable with the idea of letting go. Having a child with learning disabilities can make some parents deeply overprotective without their realizing it—even if they know that you're smart enough to move forward in life. It's not you they don't trust—it's the world in general. If you think this is the case, starting a fight over their hesitations will simply make matters worse. Enlist the assistance of a teacher or an aide, who can discuss your parents' concerns and then gently demolish those concerns.

Getting What You Deserve

FACT: You are entitled by law to the education given to any other school-age kid.

Not too long ago, schools weren't set up to handle kids with any kind of disability. If you had special needs, you had to go to a special school. It was a financial drain on parents, and it isolated students at the time when they needed most to be included. But in the mid-1970s, the federal Individuals with Disabilities Education Act (IDEA) was enacted. Run by the U.S. Department of Education, it has since become the standard for inclusion in public schools.

Simply put, IDEA states that each state must meet minimum federal standards for accommodating the needs of disabled students and that each state will be given the funds it needs from the federal government to meet those standards. Special education and related services will be provided through the school system, as needed. These services, which can include physical and speech-language therapy, are provided at no cost to you or your parents.

IDEA oversees the ways that early intervention services and special education and related services are provided to children with disabilities. Under IDEA, cerebral palsy is considered an "orthopedic impairment," which is defined as something physical "that adversely affects a child's educational performance." The term includes impairments caused by congenital anomaly (e.g., clubfoot, absence of a limb, etc.), impairments caused by disease (e.g., poliomyelitis, bone tuberculosis, etc.), and impairments from other causes (e.g., cerebral palsy, amputations, and fractures or burns that cause contractures).

It wasn't ideal—no program is—but it was a good start. And it was what made it possible for you to attend a public school.

But it's one thing to say you are entitled to the same education as anyone else. It's another thing to be able to survive it. Even on good days, the physical act of getting through school can be difficult—physical obstacles, crowds, everyone trying to get from point A to point B with a stop at their lockers in between, if there's time. There's no shame in being overwhelmed. If you need more time to get to classes, ask for it. School administrators are some of the hardest-working, most underpaid people in the country, and occasionally it may seem as though they've created red tape just to tangle you up in it, but they will work with your needs as best they can.

And if anyone gives you a hassle, or tries to claim you don't belong in a public school for any reason whatsoever, you have the law on your side. In 2000, a jury ordered a school district in Seattle, Washington, to pay $300,000 to a student with cerebral palsy who was subjected to ridicule and abuse by a fellow student, ruling that the school district had not protected the student's right to an equal, discrimination-free education.

More than that, schools—and all public facilities—are required by law to provide a physical environment in which you can function. It may be as simple as installing a water fountain that can be reached from a wheelchair, or enlarging bathroom stalls and adding handrails. It could mean installing an elevator or—if they don't have the means to do that—ensuring that all of your classes are reachable, without reducing the level of education you receive. It's part of the Americans with Disabilities Act, and it may be the most important piece of legislation in your life.

David is fifteen and is a straight-A student who works with a one-on-one aide in school to help with his writing skills. "I often ask for modifications of my work, because some tasks I cannot accomplish [as they're assigned]. If you are not vocal, then you will not get what you need in school."

He is confident in what he wants, and he knows what he needs to reach those goals. And, because of that, he often achieves them.

Schoolwork may not be the most important thing in your life right now. Life when you're a teenager doesn't really revolve around who you are; rather, it's who you know. Your friends set your social status: Are you a jock? A geek? A brain? A freak? It's cruel, and it's pretty much inescapable, no matter who you are. But you face an additional disadvantage, because even if you are a brain, a geek, a bookworm, or a rabid sports fan, you're going to be lumped under an entirely different category: disabled.

The truth is, who you are is going to change a great many times in your life. Your interests will change, your outlook will change. What you want out of life will change. You're not who you were in grade school, and you won't be the same when you're in college or out in the so-called real world. So start changing now. If you're interested in something, go for it. Don't let anyone tell you it's not appropriate for you to work stage crew, or yearbook staff, or the drama club. All right, there are a few things that just aren't practical. I suspect that you're not going to make the football team. Sorry.

But don't be afraid to try new things. People may tell you that you can't do it. Ignore them. People may make fun of you. Prove them wrong.

Getting back to that changing body chemistry, those raging hormones—yes, it's time to talk about that growing interest in dating that you may be discovering. Dating is tough enough without having the additional complication of CP to worry about. You may decide it's not worth it.

If you need help with basic daily chores, it's not surprising if you think you're never going to go on a date, never find someone you want to become intimate with.

It's entirely possible you think there isn't anyone out there who would want to be intimate with you. But you'd be very wrong.

Social worker Russell Shuttleworth conducted a study of fourteen men with moderate to severe cerebral palsy. He found that most of them have had sexual relationships or currently are in relationships with partners who find them sexually desirable. These men also noted that any physical difficulties they had with sexual activity pushed them to be more creative, not less active.

First, stop thinking about dating, about relationships, about sex as being physical. Yes, of course it is. But that's not all it is. It's about finding someone you like spending time with; someone who likes the same movies—or is willing to put up with your taste in movies so long as you'll then go see one that she enjoys; someone who thinks you're interesting, funny, smart, cute, easy to talk to.

Beth started dating Craig when they were both sophomores in high school. At first, it was just group outings—going to the movies or hanging out in the local diner after school. But they began spending more time together, just the two of them, and when he finally worked up the nerve to kiss her good night, Beth said, "It was like a lightbulb went on over my head—'Oh, right. That's where we were heading.'" Does it matter to her that Craig has difficulty speaking, and often becomes frustrated when he can't make himself understood? "Well, yeah," she admits. "I'd much rather he not have to struggle so hard to get words to come out right. And I'd love to be able to dance at the junior prom, but we won't because he's self-conscious about how his body looks, because his left side is palsied. But I love the way he hugs me, and how he listens to me. Craig's the best thing that's happened to me in my entire life, and his having cerebral palsy is part of what makes him, him."

In short, your standards should be the same as anyone's: Look for the person who sees beyond the surface, who is interested in being with you and is willing to take the extra time it takes to become comfortable with you. It sounds clichéd, but clichés are formed from proven truths.

And you just may discover that the person you were infatuated with has become a good friend—and the person you thought was simply a good friend has become something more than that. Life's bizarre that way.

Other Activities

School, home, therapy. School, home, therapy. You want more out of life than what you've got? Break that chain right now. Get involved.

And yes, you have more options in front of you than the chess club. Athletics, for one.

You may think that sports are completely out of your reach. You're wrong. True, the Olympics probably aren't in your future. They're not in mine, either. But there are a number of physical outlets that are open to you.

Earlier, we briefly discussed hippotherapy, or horseback riding, as a means of therapy. But horseback riding is also

31

a sport, and one that, if your motor skills can handle it, can be enjoyed for your entire life. Plus, there are many stables that can arrange for you to work with the horses, rather than just showing up and getting on one.

Likewise, nonteam sports like bowling, adaptive cycling, and even golf have the dual advantage of being fun and a way to meet people whom you might not ordinarily encounter. Your doctor or therapist might know of local organizations that sponsor activities, or you can call up your local Y or community organization and ask them to send you a catalog.

And if you're feeling really adventurous, why not see if skiing is for you? Yes, skiing. Many ski resorts operate on U.S. Forest Service land and are therefore required to have handicap-accessible programming, which often includes specialized ski equipment. Ask about discounted lift tickets!

The National Sports Center for the Disabled is a great place to start if you're interested in the outdoors. You can reach them by mail at P.O. Box 1290, Winter Park, Colorado, 80482, or by phone at 970-726-1540. Or, you can reach them via e-mail at info@nscd.org.

Interested in something a little more esoteric? Try golf— there are a number of organizations that will teach you how to play. Contact the Therapeutic Golf Foundation at (205) 980-1911 for further information.

Or for something really unusual, check out the Tradewinds Foundation. Tradewinds is a nonprofit marine organization founded solely to work with and support kids and adults with disabilities. It is supported and endorsed by both the Cerebral Palsy Association and

Big Brothers/Big Sisters. Not only does this organization open up the world of sailing to many people who otherwise would never have access to ships or sailboats, but it also offers vocational training to those qualified. They have offices in New York, Florida, and California.

Not into sweating, but still want to do something outdoors? Try camping! There are a number of facilities across the United States that offer just the right combination of support and freedom, out in the woods, by a lake, or up in the mountains. The American Camping Association will take your preferences into account and find the right camp for you.

Or try out for an extracurricular activity you might not have ever thought about. Book clubs are a wonderful way to meet a wide range of people, and all you have to do is go to your local bookstore to find out when the next group meets. If you're handy with a paintbrush or like to work with costumes, or even if you have an interest in learning how to run the soundboard, your local theater group would probably welcome you with open arms. Play an instrument? Sing? Check out local bands and choral groups.

"Chorus is a lot of fun and is very good for me," David says. *"I don't have a normal breathing pattern, and chorus helps that tremendously. About every two months, there is a concert. Sometimes, the concert equipment is set up so that I can't get through with my walker. Again, I know that I need to be vocal about my needs. Once I make sure that everything is okay, I am able to look the best that I can onstage."*

The real joy of participating in group activities is that once you get into it, all that matters is what you're doing. It's not you, the disabled person, and the others, the disabled people—it's a group, working toward a single goal. And, after a while, you're going to discover that nobody really thinks about it any more. You won't be "the guy in the wheelchair," or "the girl who can't lift anything with her left arm"—you'll be "Joe, who's in my debating club," or "Sarah, who sings alto." They won't forget, certainly—your cerebral palsy is not going to disappear—but it won't define who you are.

How Do I Get There from Here?

All right. You're tired of reading—you want all the things discussed in earlier chapters: a social life, a boyfriend or girlfriend, freedom, and activities that don't limit or define who you are by what you can't do. The first step to independence is self-determination. Or, to steal shamelessly from the U.S. Army—Be All You Can Be. Remember what was said back in chapter one? Never accept someone saying "You can't" when you think "Maybe I could."

But self-determination is more than simply setting goals, or even achieving them. It has to do with making sure that you're ready for those goals. In a way, it's like packing a suitcase for a trip. You want to make sure you have everything you're going to need along the way, right? That's what self-determination is: making sure you're ready emotionally for the trip ahead.

A Checklist for Self-Determination

1. Listen to your own inner voice

2. Stay centered

3. Develop a support network

4. Accept limits, but not limitations

Your inner voice isn't the urge you feel to do or say something—that's just your id, the word some psychiatrists use to describe your impulsive instinct. The inner voice is a more rational, thoughtful voice, something that rises up from deep within you and takes into consideration not just your needs, but outside influences as well. Some people call it their "good angel," or the voice of reason, a conscience or an ethical guide. It's the ability to weed out the excuses and the garbage that we all build up, and to cut to the chase.

You'll have to work hard to listen for your inner voice, and learn how to distinguish it from all the other thoughts and impulses that fill one's brain. But once you do, it may become the best aid you have. It will tell you if a course of action is right for you, if a decision is a good and reasoned one, or if you are heading in the wrong direction.

You're probably accustomed to listening to what others have to say, and taking direction from them: your parents, your doctors, your therapists, and your teachers. And listening to your inner voice doesn't mean you should stop listening to them. In fact, you may have to listen even more closely, because they're giving you the information your inner voice needs.

For all that, it's actually quite easy to "hear" your inner voice. Listen to how you feel after making a decision. Are you calm about it? Does it feel like it fits, or are there loose ends still jangling about, disturbing you? That's your inner voice talking, loud and clear.

Centering is another New Age–sounding term , but you're probably doing it already without realizing it. Centering is a form of meditation that allows you to—that's right—find your center. The simplest explanation is that you're in balance: mind, heart, and body. Very few people can live their whole lives like that, but it's an achievable goal that everyone can reach with a little practice.

Why should you try to center yourself? When you are centered, you feel calm and in control of your emotions. When you're not centered, your mind can't concentrate and your emotions run wild over your decision-making process. You'll also find that when you're centered, it becomes much easier to take tests or deal with emotionally charged or difficult situations.

It sounds complicated, but centering can be as easy as taking a deep breath. In fact, it probably feels a lot like some of the exercises your therapist may already have you doing. When you're feeling stressed-out or confused, try taking several slow, deep breaths. With each in-breath, imagine you are pulling all of your scattered energy and attention back into your body. Then exhale, letting go of any stress or negative thoughts and emotions.

Feel the weight of your body settle to where it's most comfortable: For many people, that's a spot a little forward of their spines, just above their belly buttons. But for you it may feel a little different. Don't force it where it doesn't want to go. That's your center. Let the energy pool in there, then feel it spread outward into your limbs and up your spine. You might want to practice at night before you go to bed, or wake up a few minutes earlier and practice then, before the stress of the day catches up with you. Once you've got the hang of it, you'll be able to call it up easily, no matter where you are or what you're doing.

Once you're centering and listening to your inner voice, it's time to let some other voices in. Find someone you can rely on. It may be a parent, a friend, another relative, a therapist, or teacher. All that's required is that you trust his or her opinions, even when you disagree. Then find another—someone who won't simply echo the opinions of the first person. This is the start of your support group, people you can bounce ideas, opinions, or theories off of, and trust that their responses won't have their own agenda attached to it.

And, last but certainly not least, keep in mind at all times the reality of your situation. You are not Superman or Superwoman, but you aren't helpless, either. Work with what you can do; don't long after things that are impossible. And if you think that something out of your reach now may be possible, then look logically at the steps that would make it so. Wishing and dreaming won't do it—but work and preparation might. Everyone has limits to what he or she can accomplish, but nobody can tell what they are except you.

Yes, you've spent most of your life depending on other people. But that dependency can and should—indeed it must—evolve into something less constricting, and more constructive for everyone involved. Self-determination is about redefining and re-creating yourself—sculpting the "who" you're going to be out of who you were. And you're the only person who can do it.

One of the surest signs that you've reached self-determination is the ability to handle what could be called "sucker punches," the things that come out of nowhere and leave you emotionally, if not literally, gasping for breath. Despite all of the good intentions and education in the world, there will still come a time when you have to deal with someone who thinks that having cerebral palsy makes you a fair target for his or her idea of humor, cluelessness, or bigotry. But don't become overconfident: Part of being independent is knowing when you can handle things like that and when you don't have to do so.

Insensitive Questions

Believe it or not, there is a difference between "Why do you look/talk/walk like that?" and "Why do you look/talk/walk like that?" The difference isn't in the words but in the tone of voice, the body language of the questioner, and, most of all, the intent. A person who is looking to understand you better may ask an awkward or insulting question out of ignorance, but he will learn by your response and tailor his next question better. But some people, unfortunately, are just out for the sensation, the thrill of being able to say "Look who I talked to," simply because you're different than anyone else they know. There's nothing you can do to educate them, because they're not really listening to you.

Don't get angry. Again, you won't teach them anything. Answer their questions as politely as possible and then move away. If they follow you, or otherwise insist on asking questions you don't feel comfortable answering, ask them to leave you alone. Most will give up at that point.

If they don't, it's time to call someone in authority, either a teacher or—outside the school setting—a police officer. You're being harassed. Don't put up with it.

Name-Calling and Other Forms of Bigotry

The most basic definition of bigotry is "unreasonably prejudiced and intolerant." Some of it, relatively speaking, isn't serious:

> *"Mainly what I got was harmless—they would stand near me and, when I went past, yell 'ow ow ow ow ow' like I'd run over their feet. One kid made a big deal about how much space I was taking up at the lockers."*

And some of it is:

> *"This guy used to stand outside the school, waiting for me. He'd tell me I shouldn't be allowed there, that I was just using up tax money that should be used for something important."*

You haven't reached your teens without discovering that there really are people out there whose sole purpose in life seems to be making a big pain of themselves, in as many ways as possible. And somehow you seem to land squarely in their preferred target zone.

There's nothing to be done about people like that. You can't shout them down, you can't shut them up, and all the best intentions in the world still don't make it possible to ignore them. Unfortunately, knowing that it's their own fear and ignorance that makes them talk that way doesn't make their words hurt any less. And all the self-determination, sheer stubbornness, and support from outside isn't going to stop the days when you think it's just not worth it. That's when you wonder, again, "Why me?"

Depression

Just as you should never let anyone take away your right to decide what you can do, you shouldn't ever let someone tell you that you can't wallow in misery. That, too, is a basic human right: to sit in the dark and be miserable. Just as there are days when you feel optimistic, cheerful, and otherwise annoyingly can-do-it, there will be days when the opposite is true. It could last a day; it could last a week. So long as you're able to get up and go on with your normal routine, it's okay to indulge. Everyone's allowed down time, especially if something understandable triggered it: a physical setback, a bad fight with your parents, a total misunderstanding with your friends. Even something that seems silly to others, like missing a television show you were sure the VCR was taping, is reason to be depressed.

The trick is to know when to stop. Depression can be a dangerous thing, mainly because it's so comfortable. If we expect negative things to happen, they may not—but not many positive things will occur, either. So enjoy a day or two of misery, if you feel the need, but then get back out into the world and go forward again. You will probably discover that the thing that was so horrible at the beginning may have blown over completely. You may discover a solution to the problem, overcome the setback, or find that someone else had taped that show and is willing to loan you the tape. Life goes on. Take a deep breath, find your center, call up your friends, and make something positive happen.

If, however, you find you're having difficulty shaking off the black mood, again it's time to make a noise. Tell someone. Chronic depression is always a risk for people with physical difficulties, and even more so for teenagers. And it may not be something you can just shake off without help. Look and ask. That help will be there.

As part of taking control of your life, you may want to keep up with the ever-changing medical scene as it relates to your situation. If so, you'll need access to journals, magazines, and newspapers. Many of these articles are written for the professional fields, but you'll be able to find a great deal of information written for the layperson as well.

You might also be able to access the Health Reference Center from your library. Part of Infotrac, it's a full-text database that includes excerpts and complete text from a variety of publications on all aspects of health. You will need to contact your library for this, however, since you need a password in order to get in.

Also, if you have a college or university in your town, see if it will allow you to use its facilities. Its library is more likely to have specific journals or textbooks you may need, especially if it has a strong education or biology department. And while you're doing that, check with your local library to see if you can access its databases via modem link from your home computer. It may not be widely available, but exceptions can be made. This is especially helpful if you live in a town that hasn't been able to upgrade its own equipment for you to use, or has a building that is difficult for you to navigate.

In the twenty-first century, information is quite literally at your fingertips, thanks to the Internet. Even if you don't have access at home, most public libraries have Internet connections available, and the librarians will be more than happy to help you find what it is you're looking for and will print it out for you as well!

If you've never been on the Internet before, don't worry. Rather than being a scary or an overwhelming place, it's surprisingly welcoming, with helpful road signs. And many of the better-funded libraries should have adaptive technology to ensure that you can use the computer yourself using modified keyboards, voice synthesizers, or a mouse emulator, which will allow you to use any point-and-click software, including all Internet browsers, without having someone by your side at all times. And if you do have Internet access at home, advice and encouragement is often just a click away!

After High School: What's Possible for Me?

The question isn't "What's possible?" The question is "What do you want to do?"

Once upon a time, back in the 1960s and even the 1970s, people with cerebral palsy might have had limited options once they got out of school. Even if they were able to attend a public high school, "employment for the handicapped" was limited to low-paying jobs, if they were allowed into the workforce at all. But things have changed, and for the better, in large part because of relatively new legislation which has made it illegal to discriminate against the disabled.

Thanks to that and to increasing public awareness that disabled doesn't mean incapable, you have as many choices as you'd like. You can go on to college or trade school, get a job—you have the option to do just about anything you want to do. Are there limits? Sure. Not everyone gets into every school he or she applies to. Not everyone gets the job he or she wants. But you'll never know what you can do until you try.

College

College is generally regarded as the ultimate test of independence. It's a decompression chamber. It moves you from the protected confines of your childhood home and out into the world. It's scary, even if you've been looking forward to it for years. And you have additional challenges to make it even scarier.

But at the same time, college can be a wonderful experience. Many schools take their student bodies from across the country, and often from around the world, so you're going to meet people with completely different outlooks on life. They may never have met anyone with cerebral palsy—or they may have grown up in a family where disabilities were a familiar thing. One thing will be sure: You're going to meet a lot of new people—and you aren't going to like all of them. But you may also find the person who will be your best friend for the rest of your life. And you're never going to forget a moment of the time you spend there.

Lesley is a pretty typical college freshman. She's taking all the introductory courses: "Intro to Everything," she calls it. Her roommate had called when they were first assigned a room together, and they've had a lot of conversations since then, both on the phone and online, talking about their likes and dislikes, getting to know each other before that all-important first day. But they also spent a lot of time talking about cerebral palsy, and what it was going to mean to their living arrangements. Lesley has athetoid palsy and wears leg braces in order to stand upright and walk.

"I told Jen [her roommate] that I was like the Tin Woodman before he gets the oil. So the first day of orientation, I get to the room, with my folks behind me with my stuff, and she'd placed a dozen oil cans,

all of them filled with flowers, all over the room. My mom started to cry. I knew, whatever I'd been afraid of, college was going to be okay."

Colleges generally fall into two categories: commuter, where you live at home and go to classes on campus during the day, and residential, where you live on campus during the entire session, only going home during term breaks. There are pluses and minuses to both, and the final determination may be your own comfort level.

Since college is such a radical change, many times the best choice is going to a local school so you can live at home, thereby minimizing the number of new things you'll have to get used to all at once. Once you've gotten the hang of this new life, you can always move onto campus during your sophomore year. And for some, dormitory living just isn't an option (some schools, especially in large cities, are for commuters only).

If you do want to live at school, there are things you'll have to consider, beyond the simple question of "Is this practical?" First, you will have to determine which school not only supports the programs you're interested in studying but also has a campus that suits your requirements. While every campus is by law required to be physically accessible, some are, in practical terms, better than others. In addition, some schools have programs specifically tailored for you, or a faculty with a better understanding of your needs.

Before you apply to college, be aware of the fact that you may be eligible for additional time in which to take standardized tests, such as the SAT. Such tests are currently "flagged" with the notation "scores obtained under special considerations" to indicate that the person taking them received the extra time or assistance. However, a recent court decision in California moved the Educational Testing Service to declare that they would stop flagging certain exams, such as the GRE and GMAT, effective in 2001. The SAT is owned by the College Board, and not by ETS, and as such it is not covered under that decision. The College Board has said that it will study the question, and issue a decision on the matter by March 2002.

The Workplace

Remember the Americans with Disabilities Act? It changed everything for you in the workplace. In fact, its main reason for coming into existence in 1990 was to ensure that employers could not discriminate against anyone with a disability. If you can do the job you've applied for, even if it would require reasonable flexibility on the part of the employer, you must, by law, receive equal consideration. And if you can prove that you were passed over for another equally qualified candidate merely on the basis of your physical condition, you can take that employer to court—and win.

According to the act:

> ↪ Employers may not discriminate against an individual with a disability in hiring or promotion if the person is otherwise qualified for the job.

47

⇨ Employers may ask about one's ability to perform a job, but cannot inquire if someone has a disability or subject a person to tests that tend to screen out people with disabilities.

⇨ Employers must provide "reasonable accommodation" to individuals with disabilities. This includes steps such as job restructuring and modification of equipment. Should such accommodation place "undue hardships" on the company, the company is exempt.

⇨ Employers may not discriminate against a qualified applicant or an employee because of the known disability of an individual with whom the applicant or employee is affiliated.

This law applies to all companies with more than fourteen employees in both the public and private sector, and all government organizations regardless of size. Religious organizations are allowed to require that you conform to their tenets of faith, but otherwise they must comply.

Potential reasonable accommodations include job restructuring, reassignment to a vacant position, part-time or modified work schedules, assistive technology, or aides or qualified interpreters, as needed. Accommodations of a personal nature (such as a service animal or a wheelchair) would not be the employer's responsibility.

In one well-documented example involving the U.S. government, the U.S. Postal Service refused to promote a hearing-impaired secretary because she could not answer the telephone. The Supreme Court ordered the Postal Service to promote the individual, noting that this function could be farmed out to others within the same office, and that answering telephones was not an essential function of this particular job.

Employers who fear that accommodating a worker with a disability will lower the morale of coworkers won't get much sympathy from the courts. And the claim that co-workers or customers will not wish to associate with an individual with a disability has yet to work in any defense against an ADA lawsuit.

In fact, studies conducted in 1986 and in 1992 showed that more than half of these accommodations were simple to implement and cost little or nothing, while another 15 percent cost the employer $500 or less. Also, tax credits are available to businesses who remove architectural barriers, target jobs for individuals with disabilities, or provide assistive technology or interpreters to workers with disabilities. So don't choose your future occupation based on what has been "traditionally" open to people with cerebral palsy—aim high.

All right, maybe you haven't a clue what you want to do next month, much less what you want to do for a living. Don't panic. Very few people at your age do, unless you have a particular talent for music or art or science that you want to follow. And even then, you may not know in which direction it will take you. Just remember that you can follow it anywhere it leads you. Today, people with cerebral palsy are lawyers, social workers, writers, scientists, travel agents, and librarians, to name a few.

When Connor was born, the doctor told his parents that he would probably spend his entire life in a special home where staff could take care of him.

49

Today, at thirty-three, he's just received his master's degree in social work. He intends to spend his life taking care of other people.

"My body's not in great shape. I'm never going to run the Boston Marathon, or dance the night away. Most people don't do those things anyway. What I can do is show people that even the worst-case scenario isn't always the end and that there's hope, if you're willing to work for it."

The First Apartment

The first apartment is the stuff of jokes and legends. The broken-down futon, the bookcases made of crates and planks. Odds are if you choose to get an apartment rather than live at home, it will be a little better furnished than most. You have requirements that, well, require it. But some things will remain the same. You will still have to go grocery shopping, pay the bills, and do the laundry. It's independence, and it's wonderful.

Of course, you're also going to have to deal with people who may—for all the best-intentioned and well-meaning reasons—try to convince you that living on your own isn't a good idea. Try to listen to what they're saying and consider their objections rationally. But at the same time, don't let their opinions stop you from considering the possibility.

There is a movement called Independent Living, which was started in the 1960s. It was a reaction against the "warehousing" of people who needed greater physical assistance in homes that did not offer them acceptable levels of privacy or self-determination, and that left them dependent on staff and therapists. No matter how well-run or compassionate these facilities might have been, they rarely could be considered home, especially if the residents hadn't been given a say in the matter. If you can live on your own, or with a companion animal or aide, and you want to, you are now given that choice.

The laws against discrimination come into play here, as well. According to the Fair Housing Act, a landlord is not required to make housing accessible for you, but neither can he or she:

- ⇌ Deny you an apartment simply on the basis of your having cerebral palsy, or any other disability.

- ⇌ Discriminate against a service animal, no matter what his or her pet policy may be.

- ⇌ Refuse to let you make reasonable modifications to your dwelling or common-use areas, at your expense, if necessary for the disabled person to use the housing. (Where reasonable, the landlord may permit changes only if you agree to restore the property to its original condition when you move.)

- ⇌ Refuse to make reasonable accommodations in rules, policies, practices, or services if necessary for you to use the housing.

As mentioned above, there's a lot to consider when you start looking for an apartment, well beyond the usual "Can I afford it?" and "How convenient is it to my school or job?"

Is the building suitable? You already know how to judge if the hallways are wide enough, the stairs manageable, or if the bathroom allows you room to move safely. But you also need to consider the kitchen—can you access it comfortably? Is the fire or emergency exit one you can access? And what about the exterior—is the landlord going to handle things like snow removal, raking, and any small problems that might occur? Is the landlord on site? Are there neighbors you can contact easily? It's good to be confident in your ability to handle anything that comes your way. It's better to be confident and have backup.

In buildings that were ready for first occupancy after March 13, 1991, and that have an elevator and four or more units, public and common areas must be accessible to persons with disabilities, and doors and hallways must be wide enough for wheelchairs. In addition, all units must have an accessible route into and through the unit, accessible light switches, electrical outlets, thermostats and other environmental controls, reinforced bathroom walls to allow later installation of grab bars, and kitchens and bathrooms that can be used by people in wheelchairs.

If a building with four or more units has no elevator and was ready for first occupancy after March 13, 1991, these standards apply to ground-floor units.

If you decide that an apartment of your own isn't an option for you, living at home doesn't have to feel like a step backward. Talking to your parents can open up housing possibilities you hadn't considered before. Rachael spent two years living in a dormitory at school but when she graduated, she felt better about moving back in with her parents and getting a job in her hometown. Her old room was still available, but they all agreed that she deserved more privacy. They built a simple apartment out of what had been the garage: two rooms, a bathroom, and a small kitchenette. It was spartan and certainly wouldn't win any *Architectural Digest* awards, but it had its own entrance, and it was hers. A relatively inexpensive intercom system connected the two, allowing for discussing dinner plans as well as making emergency calls.

But if you're not ready for an apartment of your own and the thought of living at home gives you the hives, you might want to check into a local group home. It may not be for you, for any of a hundred different reasons—but you may discover that there are a hundred and one reasons why it's perfect for your needs.

I Don't Know
What to Say

This chapter may be the most important one in the book. And it's not about you. It's about the people in your life: siblings, best friends, classmates, boyfriends or girlfriends, roommates, coworkers.

These are all the people around you who need to know about cerebral palsy—what's fact, what's myth, what's hurtful, and what's helpful—and who may not know how to ask, or even if they should.

> "It frustrates me sometimes," fifteen-year-old Michael says. "People are so obviously curious about what's wrong with me, but they never say anything, like it's some kind of sin to even talk about it."

In a way, that's true. Because they care about you, they may not feel comfortable asking you questions, for fear of saying the wrong thing or hurting your feelings. But, in this case, good intentions may actually be a bad thing. They need to know—and you need to be able to talk about your cerebral palsy the same way you'd talk about anything else that so deeply affects your life. That's why this chapter was included. You should read it, and then hand it over to them. Everyone needs to see the other side if there is to be any kind of communication and evolution.

So yes, they should ask questions. And you should answer them, as best you can. Not the invasive, intrusive stuff, naturally; you're entitled to your privacy as much as they are. But honest questions deserve honest answers.

Just remember that the main cause of bigotry is ignorance, and the only cures are knowledge and empathy. And those can only grow when there's communication.

The Fear of Questions

"Is it worse to stare, or to look away, like you don't see that their bodies don't work right?"

"If I ask them if they need help, are they going to get mad?"

"Is it okay to ask what happened to them?"

All of the above are real questions, things that people think, but aren't quite sure how to ask. They're not prying or morbidly curious—they just want to know how to proceed without doing or saying something that will either make you angry or embarrass them.

Short of wearing a sign that says "Yes, I have cerebral palsy, ask me about it," there's no way you can let people know that you're willing to answer questions. But if someone does come up to you, try to remember that you're an ambassador of sorts, smoothing the way for other people with cerebral palsy, or anyone with any sort of disability at all.

But as important as it is for others to be able to ask questions, it's equally as important that you be able to answer them. Think about what you might say in response to particular questions, and prepare an answer that you feel comfortable saying. And prepare a response for questions you're not comfortable answering, too. Don't say something because it's polite, or because you think it's the right thing to say, or because it's what they want to hear. Misinformation is worse than no information at all.

Carrie, whose daughter Miriam is restricted to a wheelchair, has had to witness this firsthand:

"Just because a person's body does not cooperate does not mean that these people are any different from the rest of the population. Some are very smart, some are less so, just as in the general population. Some are outgoing; some are shy. Some are big spenders; some are conservative spenders. They have the same emotions, the same dreams and desires, the same drives, the same needs. They are no different than you or me. They are often lonelier, because people are afraid to approach them. People are afraid of the unknown and of things that are different or that they do not understand. And this is made worse by being afraid of saying the wrong things."

You may have a simple answer to these questions: you want to be treated the same as anyone else. That's a great answer—except you're not like everyone else, and situations will come up in which this just doesn't work. People will notice if you're in a wheelchair, or if you have difficulty doing something because of CP. Are you okay with someone watching you, or does it make you feel flustered or uncomfortable? "Please, I'd rather you look away" is a fair answer to that question. So is "Look all you want, so long as you don't point and laugh." (Always a good guideline, no matter who is involved.) Remember, they may not be watching you because of your disability. You may have caught their eye because of the color of your hair, the sound of your laugh, or even the way you gesture with your hands or head while you talk. Assume the best of intentions and more often than not you'll be right.

"Talk about me, not my chair," says Miriam. "That's the important point, really; I am not my chair, and you won't have a terribly fun conversation with this piece of metal and rubber. But I don't mind the occasional question, especially if it sounds like it's curiosity, not a 'So what's wrong with you?' type of question."

It's okay to accept help—and it's okay to do it on your own. Your friends and family will probably figure out quickly enough what you want or need help with, and when they should stay out of it. But strangers don't have that information, and the natural inclination of someone upon seeing another person having difficulty is to offer to help. If you snap at them or become angry, you'll scare them away from ever offering anyone help again. If you want to finish whatever it was on your own, say, "Thanks, but I've got it." It's polite, and it leaves the door open for continuing the conversation, if you both wish.

Language

The comedian George Carlin has a routine called "The Seven Words You Can't Say," involving the list of words the

FCC deemed unacceptable for airing on television and radio. Some of those words have become acceptable since he first created that routine, while others will probably never be okay to use—and for good reason. Words aren't just words. They're potential weapons. They can hurt as much or more than fists or guns.

How someone talks to you is just as important as how he or she talks about you. But don't assume that someone means to say something hurtful, especially if it wasn't in a malicious or cruel context. If your friends stumble over words or appear hesitant while speaking, it may be that they aren't sure what—in these politically sensitive times—is the right word to use to avoid giving offense.

The following are some recommendations and guidelines on what to use and not use when referring to cerebral palsy and the disabled. They were developed by United Cerebral Palsy. You may have your own preferred phrases you'll want to add, or ones you dislike, which you'll choose to delete.

- Afflicted: An affliction is a terrible thing of biblical proportions, like the plague, or a horde of locusts. A better word choice would be "affected," or "a person who has cerebral palsy."

- Cerebral palsied or cerebral paralyzed: Awkward to say, and demeaning as well. You aren't cerebral palsy, you're a person with cerebral palsy—the person comes first.

- Crippled: This paints a picture no one wants to see. Just don't use this term.

➼ Disease: Cerebral palsy is a condition, not a disease.

➼ Drain and burden: Wipe these words out of your head now. Not a single caretaker has ever used those words about their loved ones, and nobody else has the right to do so.

➼ Poor: Physical disabilities have nothing to do with economic status. "Poor" implies pity and it's inappropriate.

➼ Suffers from: If someone with a disability copes with life just as well as the able-bodied people around her, then how can she be suffering? This phrase simply does not work.

➼ Unfortunate: Do not use this term to describe people with disabilities. It's unfortunate if you spill something on a new pair of slacks. It has nothing to do with a person's quality of life.

➼ Victim: A person with a disability was neither sabotaged nor was he involved in a plane, train, bus, or car accident. There is no way to rephrase this cliché.

➼ Wheelchair-bound: This gives an image of someone attached permanently to a wheelchair. All people who use wheelchairs get out of them to go to bed, and many of them are able to move and even walk short distances without their chairs. A better term here is "a person who uses a wheelchair." If someone in a wheelchair chooses to use a slang term such as "wheelie," that's her right. Nobody else should, even if she is just joking.

And remember at all times that if your friends or co-workers hear you use a term, even if it has negative con-notations, they may assume it's not actually negative at all, and therefore all right for them to use it as well. If you don't want them to pick it up, don't use it yourself, either. Use implies consent.

Dealing with Children

Adults are often hesitant to ask questions, but children have no such qualms. They will walk right up to you and ask why you're in a wheelchair, or why you talk so funny. And far too often their parents will drag them away, apologizing furiously and scolding them for bothering you. It's a terrible thing, because that teaches children that people who are different are people to be afraid of, or people to be pitied.

> "[Kids are] going to be curious," Miriam advises parents. "Let them be curious. If they have a question that you can't field, let them talk to me. Don't pull them away—being in a wheelchair isn't contagious.
> "The most fun I've had answering questions has been from kids, just because they're fascinated about everything and don't act either condescending or embarrassed about asking questions. A five-year-old daughter of a friend was totally fascinated about the joystick control to my chair and was constantly asking questions about it."

And there's a lot that you can do to help kids learn, too. If you feel comfortable with it, volunteer to speak at your local grade school or day-care center. If you can give them a structured forum in which to ask questions, with the encouragement of their teacher, you can ease their acceptance of others later. And you just may become the new hero of a child who has a physical disability, or has a sibling or parent with a disability.

Traveling with Cerebral Palsy

Public transportation is a tricky thing. Although a great many buses are now equipped with special entrances for people who need assistance, the truth is that getting on board is only half the problem. Seats are at a premium, walkways are often crowded, and getting off when it's your stop can challenge even the most agile commuter. If you know you're going to need help or extra time say so while you're standing in line, or speak up well before your stop. Give people the chance to make room.

> "I was on the bus and a woman got on. She wasn't in a wheelchair or using a cane or braces or anything, but she was obviously having problems walking. The bus was packed, no seats. I wanted to offer her a seat, but I was scared she'd be offended, that I thought she was crippled or something."

The short answer to this is that everybody wants a seat on the bus, train, or subway. If you think it's appropriate, offer. If they're not interested, they'll say "No, thank you," and you'll have done your good deed for the day.

Much the same goes for plane travel. Although every airline has a special boarding call for those who need extra time in getting settled, disembarking is often a free-for-all.

While flight attendants will typically ask anyone who requires assistance to wait until everyone else has gotten off the plane, this isn't always possible.

If you need to get off the plane quickly, whether in order to make another flight, to use the bathroom, or simply because if you don't get off that plane soon you're going to lose your mind, alert the flight attendants via the call button, preferably before they begin the landing procedures. Once on the ground, ask the people around you if you could possibly go ahead of them. Not only will most people let you, they'll help you with your bags as well.

Living with Someone

You don't want to intrude, but . . .

The trick to living with someone is to balance concern with privacy. That's difficult enough to do under ideal circumstances. Add a disability, and the stakes go up for all concerned.

Your siblings, naturally enough, don't have a choice. They were born into the family, same as you, and if you all don't play nice, your parents will come in to arbitrate. The folks lay down the laws, and everyone falls into place. A family, no matter what else, is not a democracy.

Dormitory living is a different situation. You may not have chosen to live with the people on your floor, in your suite, in your room. And they may not have ever dealt with someone with cerebral palsy before. So there will probably be a lot of uncomfortable moments, some awkward hesitations, and maybe even a few bad starts. This is where you can take charge. Let them know that you're okay with questions, that you don't mind offers of help—or that you'd really rather work things through on your own. Set the ground rules early on, and the initial settling-in period will go much more smoothly. They're looking to you for instructions.

Yes, you may run into the totally impossible or insensitive roommate. At that point, bail. Run screaming for the housing department, if needed. There's no shame in reaching the end of your rope, socially speaking.

If you're planning on living in an apartment with someone, you've probably known that person for a while, and he or she has a pretty good idea of your comfort level. But even the best of friends can discover major incompatibilities when sharing an apartment. Even simple arguments can escalate, and words can be said that hurt badly on both sides.

In the interests of keeping things cool, agree on a cool-out signal. If things are getting too hot, say the code word and go into your separate corners until you've thought things through.

"Ginny and I had been friends for years," Tory says. "I figured, once you've held someone's head while they threw up, you've seen them at their worst, right? So we'd be able to deal with sharing an apartment, especially one as nice as this: ground floor, wide hallways my chair could zoom through, a bathroom and kitchen the landlord had redone to meet disability standards. But we had really different habits I hadn't thought of, silly stuff like where we put the milk in the fridge. And when I couldn't reach the milk one morning, and spilled it all over myself because of that, we just exploded."

63

Ginny and Tory managed to mend their friendship, and they even laugh about that milk argument now. But that moment of shame Ginny felt, and her anger, as though her friend had put the carton purposely out of reach—that was a terrible moment for both of them.

Walk through your daily routine to smooth out any rough spots. Organize shared spaces together. And above all, remember to give each other space.

Loving Someone

At this stage, your sweetie knows you, knows what you need or want help with, and when you just want to muddle through on your own. But nobody's a mind reader, and there will be times that the lines of communication get tangled. Being in a relationship like this can be a tricky thing, and both of you have to remember not to make assumptions.

But with physical intimacy comes additional problems. You want to take on your loved one's problems, make life as easy for him or her as possible. And when that loved one has cerebral palsy, that desire only increases, sometimes to the point of smothering the person. Unlike your parents, who have had years to come to work out an accommodation between the desire to help and an understanding of your needs, a boyfriend/girlfriend/lover/significant other is relatively new to the situation. He or she is going to step on your toes more than once.

It might not be a bad idea, if you think the relationship is going to be one that lasts, to talk to a counselor or adviser about finding those boundaries. You've got more on your plate than do most couples, and there's no shame in asking for professional help.

Here are three rules that work for any couple, regardless of physical problems: Keep the lines of communication open. Reassure your partner as to the desirability of his/her body. And never treat your partner as anything other than a competent adult.

Working with Cerebral Palsy

Put yourself in the average office worker's place for a minute. Offering someone assistance in an office setting is quite possibly the most difficult thing you can do. On the one hand, if you see that a coworker is having difficulty managing his coffee cup, or opening a door, the most natural thing in the world is to offer help. But you don't want to insult him, or injure his pride.

"I was concerned when Jennifer started working in the office," admitted Steven, an insurance salesman. "I mean, I knew she could do the job—she wouldn't have been hired, otherwise. But we're all in one office, and the desks are jammed in pretty tight. I was concerned she'd be too intrusive, take up too much space, and cause bad feelings.

"In the end, we had to rearrange the way we'd been working to deal with that. And yeah, there was some resentment. But she dealt with it right away, didn't try to ignore it, or pretend it wasn't a big deal. And once she's been so frank about it, how could anyone stay mad?"

The easiest answer is the one recommended earlier with regard to using public transit. Use your common sense and good manners. How would you want to be treated? If a person is having difficulty, offer aid. It might be as simple as holding a door open for her, or as detailed as helping to move the office furniture around so she can reach the phone, computer, or filing cabinet better. If you see something that is a problem—the coffee machine is placed badly, or the copier room doesn't allow enough comfortable space for a wheelchair—suggest to whoever runs the office that he has these things changed. It may be the office manager, the store supervisor, or the human resources department if you're working in a larger company.

But above all, before you think or do or suggest anything, take your attitude from Steven's comments: Your coworker has the job because he or she was the best person interviewed for the job. No matter where you work—an office, a mom-and-pop store, or a multinational corporation—a positive, helpful attitude will give him or her the best working conditions anyone could ever want.

Getting Visible: Assertiveness Without Aggression

Perhaps the most common complaint teenagers with cerebral palsy have, beyond their parents' inability to let go, is that they're not treated equally in public situations. They're not talking about discrimination of an actionable sort, however. Those have a definite definition and legal recourse. This problem is much more common—and more difficult to counter. It's the dreaded invisibility syndrome.

Restaurants and Stores

Too often (i.e., most of the time), people seem to equate a physical disability with a mental disability. When we would visit our daughter at college, we would take our daughter and her friend, another bright but disabled student who uses a wheelchair, out to lunch. People inevitably addressed me and my husband with questions about what the two would like. "Would they like to sit at this table?" "What would they like to order?" "Would they like . . . " We get this everywhere we go. It is maddening—both were right there, both were women and not children, so why do they ask us instead of them?

Waitstaff are trained to be helpful, mainly because their tips depend on it. But all too often, they're not sure how to treat someone with a physical difficulty, and so they overcompensate on the side of caution. To someone perfectly able to make decisions on his own, this comes across as annoying or patronizing, neither of which bode well for the patron's digestion, or the waitperson's tip! Not surprisingly, an informal survey proved that the higher-end the restaurant, the more likely that the staff has been trained for this situation, while casual, chain restaurants are more likely to be unprepared. But even the ritziest, most expensive restaurant in the most cosmopolitan area can have a waiter who simply cannot bring himself or herself to acknowledge you.

If you encounter this attitude, you have three choices. The first, and easiest, is to say nothing, and stiff the waitperson. It's a small revenge, but a satisfying one. But, in the end, it doesn't change anything. You still feel slighted, your companion is probably furious, and the situation at that restaurant will continue when the next disabled person comes along.

Your second option is to show by example. If the question is posed to your able-bodied companion, have him or her defer the question to you, making sure your server's attention is directed to the proper person:

"I don't know—where do you want to sit?"
Or: "Laura Anne, your turn to order!"

It's subtle, but most good servers will pick up on it. Some may even apologize. Remember, it's not that they mean to be insensitive or rude. They simply may not be certain how to interact with you. It's your responsibility to inform them.

The third option is more confrontational, and you may not feel up to it. But if there comes a day when you've had enough with the invisible treatment, then step forward and demand equal treatment, with as much force as needed. "You could always ask me directly—I've found that saves time" will often not only embarrass the server in question, it will stay in his or her memory for a long time. And if that doesn't get a satisfactory response, don't be afraid to call for his or her manager and explain the problem. Don't be accusatory; merely indicate that you are not accustomed to being treated like a second-class anything, especially when you are paying for a service. That will typically guarantee that guidelines are set up for servers in the future, to prevent incidents of that sort.

Public Transportation

Public transportation has made great strides in being handicapped-accessible; unfortunately, as a general rule, people haven't. Another informal survey indicates that women and teenagers of both genders are more likely to give up their seats if they see someone who obviously needs to sit down, while adult males tend to guard their seats more tenaciously, especially if the person in need is a teenager. If you need to sit down, make that need public. "I'm really sorry, but could I sit there, please?" is really the only way to handle it. Once it's brought directly to his attention, it takes a person of astonishing selfishness to say no. And if he does, the odds are good that someone else will offer you her seat, if only to show the first person what she thinks of him.

The real problem, however, is not finding a seat, but getting on in the first place. Planes have early boarding for people who need extra time, but buses, trains, and ferries don't. And, once again, you may discover that you have suddenly become invisible while people jockey to get in line. The temptation to roll over someone's foot or "accidentally" jab someone with a brace may be overwhelming. Don't do it. A gentle "Excuse me, could you let me through?" will work much better on the majority of people, and the person who ignores you is likely to push back if shoved.

When there's a real problem, or if you run the risk of missing your transportation, alert the driver or conductor. He or she will open a way for you, ensuring that people move aside or otherwise allow you access.

On a long-haul bus ride such as on a Greyhound or Trailways bus, let the ticket-taker or driver know if you need an easy-access seat. Often the driver will keep the first seat directly behind his or her wheel open for someone with disabilities, so you don't have to make your way down the aisle. Amtrak also makes allowances for physical needs. At least one coach car has an area to accommodate individuals who wish to remain in their wheelchairs and a place to fold and store wheelchairs for those who want to use regular seats. Their overnight cars also have accessible bedrooms, including ones with room not only for a wheelchair but an aide as well. They also have some of the best restrooms ever designed for public use, complete with handrails and space to park a wheelchair without inconveniencing anyone else.

When traveling on a subway or other "connected car" transport like a monorail or train, don't be afraid to get someone's attention if you're having trouble. The conductor can and will make sure the doors remain open long enough for you to get safely inside or to get through a crowded car to reach your exit.

And if the people around you simply will not move, there's nothing better than an irritated conductor on a PA system lambasting the people getting in your way. Again, it can be embarrassing, but people will not only listen, they may learn.

Family and Social Events

Unfortunately, you can't use a PA system at family events or at a party. So when Aunt Martha asks your mother how you're doing in school when you're standing right next to her, you're on your own. Again, you have options.

Your first option: Stare them down. People never like to think they're insensitive, especially to members of their own family. Giving someone a pointed look or a raised eyebrow or some other silent indication of misbehavior is wonderfully effective, especially when used on people who are older than you are. It puts you on the moral high ground and makes the point without having to say a word. Of course, it also requires a person to be looking at you at the time, which is often the start of the problem: You're invisible. Again, running over a person's toes may start to feel justifiable. It's not.

The second option is to face people directly. This is more confrontational, and you should be careful how you use it, especially on older relatives. However, in certain situations, it's remarkably effective.

> "My grandmother never quite got over the reality that I have a severe learning disability. The fact that I'm in a regular class, that I'm just as smart, just as capable as her other grandchildren, doesn't really get through to her. She's not mean or anything—in fact, she's really sweet, but it's always in a poor little girl kind of way. I'm sixteen and I hate it. Problem is, when I get mad, my words get all jumbled and they don't sound right.
>
> "So one weekend, my mom took me and grand-mother out for lunch, and then had my dad call her away on the cell phone. So it was just me and grand-mother, and I got to tell her what was on my mind. She couldn't leave, not without abandoning me, and there wasn't anyone else she could turn to, or try to change the subject with. I don't know how much she really understood, but at least I got her to stop talking to me like I was seven. I'll take what I can get."

In Ally's case, she had her mother's involvement and assistance, not only in setting the confrontation up, but also in rehearsing what she wanted to say. You can use this method on friends as well. Choose a nonconfrontational place—a favorite pizza place or park—and focus on a specific target. This isn't the time to bring up old arguments or unrelated problems. Simply point out to your friend what she has been doing and how it's making you feel. This is probably all you're going to need to say. Even if she doesn't think she has been acting that way, you've made your point, and hopefully she will be more aware of it in the future.

Other Information You Might Need

The one point this book has tried to make is that there's very little that having cerebral palsy should keep you from trying. Brian is living proof of that.

"I was born with CP. When I was diagnosed eight months later, doctors said that I would be confined to a wheelchair for life. Even though my parents were told this, they put me in physical therapy. I went for fourteen years before the therapists said that they couldn't do any more for me. That's when I decided to take it upon myself to improve. At that time, I could barely take five steps. I made a goal to walk up and receive my diploma at high-school graduation. I started to lift weights and practice walking, and by the end of my junior year, I could walk up to a mile, although it was very wild. Then I heard about a biofeedback program in Florida that would help me learn to control my muscles. My parents and I decided to see if it would help. I went for three weeks last April and improved my walking 200 percent. So, this past June, I got to realize my goal."

This book has touched on some of the information you may need today, and in the next few years. But every person's needs are different, so all the answers you needed may not be here. And I can pretty much guarantee that you're going to have different questions next month, or next year, than you do now. Part of living is growing beyond what was into what might be, and making it into reality.

In the very beginning of the book, I told you that this was simply a starting point, a place to gather your courage before taking that next step. But you don't have to take that next step alone. There are books out there that may have answers to questions you haven't thought of yet, solutions to problems you've not encountered yet, and friendly voices letting you know you're not alone.

Unlike people in your situation fifty or even twenty years ago, organizations exist to give you advice and aid when you need it, in whatever form you need it, to create that reality. And they're local, national, and international, available by picking up a phone, writing a letter, or going online.

Try. There are never any guarantees that you'll succeed, but then, life doesn't come with guarantees for anyone.

Glossary

accommodations Techniques and materials that allow individuals to complete school or work tasks with greater ease and effectiveness.

Apgar score A numbered score that doctors use to assess a baby's physical state at birth.

apraxia Impaired ability to carry out purposeful movements in an individual who does not have significant motor problems.

assistive technology Equipment that enhances your ability to perform a task.

attention deficit disorder (ADD) A severe difficulty in focusing and maintaining attention. Also called attention deficit hyperactivity disorder (ADHD).

brain injury The physical damage to brain tissue or structure that occurs before, during, or after birth and that is verified by EEG, MRI, CAT, or a similar examination, rather than by observation of performance. When caused by an accident, the damage may be called traumatic brain injury (TBI).

congenital Present at birth.

contracture A condition in which muscles become fixed in a rigid, abnormal position causing distortion or deformity.

developmental aphasia A severe language disorder that is presumed to be because of brain injury rather than to a developmental delay.

diplegia A form of cerebral palsy in which both arms and both legs are affected, the legs being more severely so.

dyscalculia A severe difficulty in understanding and using symbols or functions needed for success in mathematics.

dysgraphia A severe difficulty in producing handwriting that is legible and written at an age-appropriate speed.

dyslexia A severe difficulty in understanding or using one or more areas of language, including listening, speaking, reading, writing, and spelling.

dysnomia A marked difficulty in remembering names or recalling words needed for oral or written language.

dyspraxia A severe difficulty in drawing, writing, buttoning, and other tasks requiring fine motor skill, or in sequencing the necessary movements.

hemianopia Defective vision or blindness that impairs half of the normal field of vision.

hemiparetic tremors Uncontrollable shaking affecting the limbs on the spastic side of the body with spastic hemiplegia.

hemiplegia (hemiparesis) A form of cerebral palsy in which spasticity affects the arm and leg on only one side of the body.

palsy Paralysis, or problems in the control of voluntary movement.

paraplegia (paraparesis) A form of cerebral palsy in which spasticity affects both legs but not the arms.

paresis (plegia) Weakness or paralysis. In cerebral palsy, typically used with another word to describe the distribution of paralysis and weakness, e.g., paraparesis.

perceptual handicap Difficulty in accurately processing, organizing, and discriminating among visual, auditory, or tactile information.

quadriplegia (quadriparesis) A form of cerebral palsy in which all four limbs are affected equally.

rh incompatibility A blood condition in which antibodies in a pregnant woman's blood attack fetal blood cells, impairing the fetus's supply of oxygen and nutrients.

rigidity The term is used to describe an involuntary increase in resistance of a muscle to passive stretch.

rubella Also known as German measles. A viral infection that can damage the nervous system in the developing fetus.

self-advocacy The development of specific skills and understandings that enable children and adults to explain their specific learning disabilities to others and to cope positively with the attitudes of peers, parents, teachers, and employers.

service animal A domesticated animal trained to assist in daily tasks. Typically a dog, but other animals have also been used, including but not limited to monkeys and birds.

spasticity A state in which the muscles are in a persistent state of increased involuntary reflex activity in response to a stretch.

specific language disability A severe difficulty in some aspect of listening, speaking, reading, writing, or spelling, although skills in the other areas are age-appropriate. Also called Specific Language Learning Disability (SLLD).

specific learning disability The official term used in federal legislation to refer to difficulty in certain areas of learning, rather than in all areas of learning. Synonymous with learning disabilities.

stereognosia Difficulty perceiving and identifying objects by touch.

strabismus Misalignment of the eyes.

tone Passive resistance to stretch offered by a muscle group to external manipulation. Hypertonia means that they have an above-average level of tone. Hypotonia means they have a below-average level of tone. Atonia means being without tone. Atonia is usually present in ataxia.

transition Commonly used to refer to the change from secondary school to postsecondary programs, work, and independent living typical of young adults.

Where to Go for Help

General Organizations and Associations

United States

Coalition on Sexuality and Disability
122 E. 23rd Street
New York, NY 10010
(212) 242-3900
(212) 677-6474
For answers and information, both general and specific to your own situation.

Independent Living Research Utilization Project (ILRU)
The Institute for Rehabilitation and Research
2323 South Sheppard, Suite 1000
Houston, TX 77019
(713) 520-0232
e-mail: ilru@bcm.tmc.edu
Web site: http://www.ilru.org
If you're looking for options or support, this is the place to check first. If they don't know the answer, they can help you find it.

March of Dimes Birth Defects Foundation
1275 Mamaroneck Avenue
White Plains, NY 10605
(914) 428-7100
(888) MODIMES (663-4637)
Web site: http://www.modimes.org
One of the more publicly visible of the advocacy organizations,
working with all types of birth-related disabilities.

National Easter Seals Society/Easter Seals
230 West Monroe Street, Suite 1800
Chicago, IL 60606-4802
(312) 726-6200
(800) 221-6827
Web site: http://www.easter-seals.org
Another well-known advocacy organization, this one focuses
on a variety of disabilities.

United Cerebral Palsy
1600 L Street NW, Suite 700
Washington, DC 20036
(202) 776-0406
(800) 872-5827
e-mail: webmaster@ucp.org
Web site: http://www.ucp.org
One of the best known and best organized advocacy
organizations for cerebral palsy, with chapters in almost
every state.

Canada

Cerebral Palsy Canada
Web site: http://www.cerebralpalsycanada.com/index.htm
Advice, interaction, and resources, with offices in
all the provinces.

Alberta
Cerebral Palsy Association in Alberta
8180 Macleod Trail South, Suite 10
Calgary, AB T2H 2B8
(403) 543-1161
(800) 363-2807 (in Alberta)

British Columbia
Cerebral Palsy Association of B.C.
15-3683 E. Hastings Street
Vancouver, BC V5K 4Z7
(604) 205-9455

Manitoba
Cerebral Palsy Association of Manitoba
825 Sherbrook Street
Winnipeg, MB R3A 1M5
(204) 774-9427

New Brunswick
New Brunswick Cerebral Palsy Foundation
P.O. Box 2152
Saint John, NB E2L 3V1

Newfoundland
Newfoundland Cerebral Palsy Association
P.O. 23059, Churchill Square Postal Outlet
St. John's, NF A1B 4J9
(709) 753-9922

Nova Scotia
Halifax Regional Cerebral Palsy Association
Box 33075, Quinpool Postal Station
Halifax, NS B3L 4T6
(902) 423-8345

Ontario
Ontario Federation for Cerebral Palsy
1630 Lawrence Avenue West, Suite 104
Toronto, ON M6L 1C5
(416) 244-9686

Prince Edward Island
P.E.I. Cerebral Palsy Association
P.O. Box 2702, 161 St. Peter's Road
Charlottetown, PE C1A 8C3
(902) 892-9694

Quebec
Association de Paralysie Cerebrale du Quebec
4810 Rue de Rouen
Montreal, QC H1V 3T4
(514) 257-4341

Saskatchewan
Saskatchewan Cerebral Palsy Association
2310 Louise Avenue
Saskatoon, SK S7J 2C7
(306) 955-7272

Specific Organizations and Associations

Epilepsy

Epilepsy Foundation
4351 Garden City Drive, Suite 406
Landover, MD 20785-7223
(301) 459-3700
(800) EFA-1000 (332-1000)
Web site: http://www.epilepsyfoundation.org

Hearing Impairments
National Institute on Deafness and Other
    Communication Disorders
National Institutes of Health
31 Center Drive, MSC 2320
Bethesda, MD 20892-2320
Web site: http://www.nidcd.nih.gov

Learning Disabilities
Learning Disabilities Association
4156 Library Road
Pittsburgh, PA 15234-1349
(412) 341-1515
e-mail: ldanatl@usaor.net
Web site: http://www.ldanatl.org

National Center for Learning Disabilities
381 Park Avenue South, Suite 1401
New York, NY 10016
(212) 545-7510
(888) 575-7373
Web site: http://www.ncld.org

CHADD: Children and Adults with
    Attention-Deficit/Hyperactivity Disorder
8181 Professional Place, Suite 201
Landover, MD 20785
(301) 306-7070
Web site: http://www.chadd.org

Scoliosis
The Scoliosis Association, Inc.
P.O. Box 265
Lake Forest, CA 92630-0265 (or)

P.O. Box 811705
Boca Raton FL 33481-1705
(800) 800-0669
e-mail: normlipin@aol.com
Web site: http://www.scoliosis-assoc.org

Transportation

Access Mobility Systems
21104 70th Avenue W.
Edmonds, WA 98026
(425) 771-4659
Web site: http://www.accessams.com

Freedom Wheelchair Lifts, Inc.
1084 Katy Road
Keller, TX 76248
(817) 431-9437
Web site: http://www.vansrus.com

Rainbow Wheels
804A Eyrie Drive
Oviedo, FL 32765
(800) 910-VANS (8267)
Web site: http://www.rainbowwheels.com

Visual Impairments

The New York Institute for Special Education
999 Pelham Parkway
Bronx, New York 10469
(718) 519-7000 Ext. 315
Web site: http://www.nyise.org

Web Sites

Support Groups

Ability Online—A free online community
http://www.ablelink.org

Cerebral Palsy Information Central
http://www.geocities.com/HotSprings/Sauna/4441/index2.htm

Cerebral Palsy Web Forum—A Web-based bulletin board on
    all aspects of CP.
http://neuro-www.mgh.harvard.edu/forum
    CerebralPalsyMenu.html

United States

Center for Information Technology Accommodation
http://www.itpolicy.gsa.gov/cita

Cerebral Palsy File: Center for Current Research
http://www.lifestages.com/health/cerebral.html

Council for Exceptional Children
http://www.ericec.org

Institute for Independent Living
http://www.independentliving.org

National Sports Center for the Disabled
http://www.nscd.org/

Quackwatch—medical scams and reliable information
http://www.quackwatch.com

United States Cerebral Palsy Athletic Association
http://www.uscpaa.org

U.S. Department of Justice: Americans with Disabilities Act
http://www.usdoj.gov/crt/ada/adahom1.htm

Canada and Worldwide

Canadian Cerebral Palsy Sports Association
http://www.ccpsa.ca

Cerebral Palsy Association of Western Australia
http://members.iinet.net.au/~cpawa

Scope: Support and Services for People with
    Cerebral Palsy (UK-based)
http://www.scope.org.uk/help/contents.shtml

For Further Reading

Nonfiction, Advice, and Research

Carter, Alden R. *Stretching Ourselves: Kids with Cerebral Palsy.* Morton Grove, IL: Albert Whitman & Co., 2000.

Dybwad, Gunnar, and Hank Bersani, eds. *New Voices, Self-Advocacy by People with Disabilities.* Cambridge, MA: Brookline Books, 1996.

Kravets, Marybeth, and Imy F. Wax, eds. *The K & W Guide to Colleges for the Learning Disabled.* 4th ed. New York: Harper Perennial, 1999.

Mangrum, Charles T., and Stephen S. Strichart, eds. *Peterson's Colleges with Programs for Students with Learning Disabilities.* 5th ed. Princeton, NJ: Peterson's Guides, 1997.

Nixon, Shelley. *From Where I Sit: Making My Way with Cerebral Palsy.* New York: Scholastic Books, 1999.

Pincus, Dion. *Everything You Need to Know About Cerebral Palsy.* New York: The Rosen Publishing Group, 1999.

Thomas, Andrew P., Martin Bax, and Diane Smyth. *The Health and Social Needs of Young Adults with Physical Disabilities.* New York: Lippincott-Raven Publishers, 1991.

Fiction

Metzger, Lois. *Barry's Sister.* New York: Puffin Books, 1993.

Films

My Left Foot
Directed by Jim Sheridan (1989)
Starring Daniel Day Lewis. Writer Christy Brown, an Irish-born
　　quadriplegic, wrote the autobiography on which the film
　　is based.

Gaby: A True Story
Directed by Luis Mandoki (1987)
Starring Liv Ullman and Robert Loggia.

Index

A

American Camping
    Association, 33
Americans with Disabilities Act,
    28, 47, 49
anger, 2, 3, 39
animals, service, 24–26, 48, 51
Apgar score, 7
assertiveness, 67–73
ataxic, 9
athetoid, 9, 45
attention deficit disorder
    (ADD), 12
attention deficit hyperactivity
    disorder (ADHD), 12
audio processing disorders, 12

B

babies, 7, 8
balance, 9, 17
Beethoven, Ludwig van, 4
bicycling, 17
Biden, Joseph, 4
Big Brothers/Big Sisters, 33
bigotry, 39, 40–41, 55
birth defects, 7
bitterness, 2
bladder control, 10
blame, 2
botox, 17
bowel control, 10
bowling, 32
brain, 5, 8, 9, 11
breaking down barriers, 7, 29
breathing, proper, 37
breathing problems, 10

C

Callahan, John, 4
camping, 33
Carlin, George, 57
Carroll, Lewis, 4
centering, 35, 37
cerebral palsy
    basic facts, 5–19
    causes and symptoms, 7–8
    cures, lack of, 18
    defined, 5–7
    in infants, 14
    introduction to, 1–4
    management of, 14–19
    statistics, 2, 11
    types of, 9–11
Cerebral Palsy Association, 32
children, dealing with, 60–61
Churchill, Winston, 4
Close, Chuck, 4
clubs, 33
cohabitation, 62–64
college, 44–47
College Board, 47
communication, 15, 54–60,
    64, 65
communication disorders, 12
Cronkite, Walter, 4

D

damage, pre- or postnatal, 8
dating, 29–31
deformed limbs, 7
depression, 41–42
depth perception, 9, 16
developmental aphasia, 12

diplegia, 10
discrimination, 44, 47–48, 51
doctors, 14, 19, 36
dormitory living, 62–63
drug therapy, 15
dyscalculia, 12, 13
dyslexia, 12

E
education, 7, 26–29
Educational Testing Service, 47
electrical stimulation, 18
employment, 44, 47–50, 65–66
epilepsy, 8
exercise, 18

F
Fair Housing Act, 51
family and social events, 71–73
Feldenkrais, 16
Feldenkrais Guild, 16
Fonseca, Chris, 4
friends, 29, 38, 54

G
genome typing, 5
golf, 32
group homes, 53

H
Hawking, Stephen, 4
Health Reference Center, 42
hearing problems, 8, 10, 16
Heller, Joseph, 4
help, accepting, 57, 66
hemiplegia, 10
hippotherapy (horseback riding),
        16–17, 31–32

Hockenberry, John, 4
Hyberbaric Oxygen Therapy
        (HBO/HBOT), 18

I
independence, 21–26, 35, 44, 50
Independent Living, 50–51
Individuals with Disabilities
        Education Act (IDEA),
        26–27
infection, 8
Infotrac, 42
inner voice, 35–37, 38
insensitive questions, 39–40
Internet, 2, 14, 42–43

J
Jones, James Earl, 4
Journal of Pediatrics, 12

K
Keller, Helen, 4
Kovic, Ron, 4

L
language, 57–60
learning disabilities, 6, 8, 10,
        11–14
love, 64–65

M
Matlin, Marlee, 4
meditation, 37
mental impairment, 11
mixed (type of cerebral palsy), 9
monoplegia, 10
motor function, 5
movement, involuntary, 9

About the Author

Laura Anne Gilman is a freelance writer and editor.

Acknowledgments

I would like to thank Betsy Vera, Carrie and Miriam Rocke, Lynn and David Bolyn, Josepha Sherman, Ashley McConnell, GraceAnne DeCandido, and Dr. Andrea Thau.

I couldn't have written this book without the aid of the many people who replied to my questions and shared their experiences with me. Both for those who are named and those who wished to remain anonymous, I'd like to pause a moment and say thank-you—you're among some of the most amazing people it's ever been my pleasure to meet.